Gratitude Keeper ™

VOLUME 1

Gratitude Keeper™

A YEAR OF INSPIRATION, ONE DAY AT A TIME

Dr. Maxine McLean IMD, DHS. Ph.D

Scripture taken from the Holy Bible, NEW INTERNATIONAL VERSION®. Copyright © 1973, 1978, 1984, 2011 by Biblica, Inc. All rights reserved worldwide. Used by permission. NEW INTERNATIONAL VERSION® and NIV® are registered trademarks of Biblica, Inc. Use of either trademark for the offering of goods or services requires the prior written consent of Biblica US, Inc.

Balboa Press books may be ordered through booksellers or by contacting:

Balboa Press
A Division of Hay House
1663 Liberty Drive
Bloomington, IN 47403
www.balboapress.com
1 (877) 407-4847

Because of the dynamic nature of the Internet, any web addresses or links contained in this book may have changed since publication and may no longer be valid. The views expressed in this work are solely those of the author and do not necessarily reflect the views of the publisher, and the publisher hereby disclaims any responsibility for them.

Any people depicted in stock imagery provided by Thinkstock are models, and such images are being used for illustrative purposes only.
Certain stock imagery © Thinkstock.

ISBN: 978-1-5043-7821-5 (sc)
ISBN: 978-1-5043-7822-2 (e)

Library of Congress Control Number: 2017905462

Print information available on the last page.

Balboa Press rev. date: 05/11/2017

BALBOA.
PRESS
A DIVISION OF HAY HOUSE

Author and Artistic Director
Maxine McLean

Artistic Design
Maxine McLean

Cover Design and Layout
Zohra Karim

Layout Director
Zohra Karim

Logo Design and Layout
Sean Ceaser
and Andrew Buchanan

Videographer/Edit
Andrew Buchanan

Publisher
Hay House and Balboa

For information, please contact Maxine McLean at <u>drmaxinemclean@gmail.com</u>

Gratitude
Keeper

Dedication with Love and Gratitude

A heartfelt gratitude! To all the supporters and contributors of this project, thank you for sharing this vision.

I am grateful for the loyalty and commitment of my family and friends, from whence I received in abundance: understanding, love, and support. To women in all parts of the world and the women of Tabaka and Kambere Village in Kenya; you're all my inspiration. You have made my journey of gratitude more meaningful and purpose-driven.

Daily you strive for clean drinking water that is supposed to be a blessing and so abundant in many parts of the world. For ten hours, you labor to the dam in the unrelenting heat of the sun and compete with the crocodiles living in the dam just to have water for your family.

Your labor is not in vain. Women and men just like me are here for you. We may not see you on your journey, feel your pain, or hear you when you cry for help, but we know you are there.

We are doing all we can to help ease that burden for you. It is our hope that through the design and outreach of Gratitude Keeper a remarkable difference will unfold on your side of the world and in each of your lives.

Maxine Mclean PhD, (IMD, DHS)

As we experience life, there
is always that which will
inspire us each step of the
way; if we only but listen.
~Maxine McLean

Introduction

Have you spent any me time thinking about your life from different perspectives? Why? Because perspective opens the door to gratitude, and this changes everything. With the right perspective, gratitude is absolutely at the core of successful living.

This Gratitude Keeper approach and the design of practicing it is immensely powerful. It will assist you on your life journey and perhaps transform your lifestyle, your perspective on life, and your health on all levels—physical, emotional, and spiritual.

Gratitude Keeper will nourish you; moreover, it will dispense a powerful essence on the people you love. You can pass your completed Gratitude Keeper on to your children, who only need to read your notes to understand and be motivated by your transformation through practicing positivity and gratitude.

It's a wonderful way to share all your treasured insights of gratitude with the people you care about most. You will inspire them to pursue true enlightened consciousness of love and gratitude, which will explicitly ripple on through to future generations.

- *Thinking positive* … stimulates the neuropeptides in your brain, which go on a journey throughout your body.
- *Writing it out* … affirms it.
- *Placing it in your gratitude book* … reinforces it.
- *Passing it on as a family heirloom* … releases it, outlaying ripples of positive vibrations—creating an impressive impact!

The idea of being thankful is not a new approach, and throughout parts of the world, people give thanks divergently through varied celebrations. Gratitude Keeper was first designed to assist in one's personal journey.

Hence, this daily practice may hold powerful vibrations for you and perhaps the key to reboot your mind, invigorate your spirit, and better your health.

When Gratitude Keeper was first incepted, the inspiration to design and expand it to benefit people in developing areas of the world was strong and exhilarating. The marvel of it all was to organize a venture that would assist in a way that allowed them the ability to add their creative value to make it a win-win experience and to foster ongoing dignity in their achievements for themselves, family, and community.

Gratitude Keeper has connected with villagers from developing parts of the world who are in need of strengthening their home base and improving their lives. This connection enables them to make Gratitude Keeper boxes out of soapstone, which, in turn, provide them with sustainable income. When each Gratitude Keeper Kit is sold, a portion is contributed back to the village to assist in building sustainable wells and viable means for their education, health care, and other lifestyle necessities.

The material soapstone was chosen instead of wood because of its beauty, durability, and healing properties. Soapstone has been studied to provide electromagnetic protection. It's also a featured gift from Mother Earth's many years of vibrations and serves as an exquisite conversion to Gratitude Keeper Kits—its newfound use.

It's kind of a soft stone that is easy to carve, and when painted, it can be featured as a beautiful art accent to complement any décor, in your office or home. Moreover, it's a reminder that a portion

of your purchase contributes to the Gratitude Keeper journey in blessing the lives of others near and far.

Therefore, each Gratitude Keeper box is carved out of soapstone. There is no doubt that soapstone has been in existence for more years than we can envision. It has embodied earth's energies and absorbed the calls of nature and the whispers of the universe.

Hence, each Gratitude Keeper box has been inscribed with the name of a trailblazer, one who has graced this earth with his or her physical presence and energy and thus influenced our paths and has imparted powerful teachings that remain a valuable asset to the journey of life.

Attached is a healing stone in its purest form; a fifteen-milliliter vial of essential oil, extracted from healing plants from nature; 365 daily Gratitude Keeper cards; and a Gratitude Keeper pen.

Your Gratitude Keeper box plus your efforts and commitment will give you all that you require to begin this journey.

Throughout these pages that follow, I have shared my experiences in the form of short stories with gratitude at the core. Mingled in are inspirational quotes, affirmations, breath work, and meditations. Therefore, no matter where you are in your life's journey or circumstance, be prepared. You are destined to have an awakening and a definable life-changing experience.

Contents

Gratitude Keeper

Chapter 1
How to Use Your Gratitude Keeper

Every day, morning or evening (whatever time of day feels best for you), sit or stand in a comfortable position and close your eyes (to prevent distractions). Now take three full breaths in through your nostrils and down into that space between your pubic bone and your navel. As you breathe that air, sense the full expansion of your abdomen (belly). Hold this breath for the count of three, and then gently and fully release.

As you release each breath, sense the upward flow of air as your abdomen contracts; exhale through pursed lips. Stay conscious of your breathing as the movement of your breath flows effortlessly. Follow the rhythm; don't rush the flow. Relax in the moment. This will become easier with practice and time.

Now take your awareness to your entire body—from the top of your head to the tips of your toes. After the third full inhalation, you may return to your normal breathing pattern. Discern the quietness around you.

In this quiet space, take a few minutes to think of one thing—and only one thing—that you are grateful for, just for today, just for this moment. (Don't try to analyze it, and don't question it.) Then, simply allow your thoughts to flow freely to embrace that one thing.

Write that one thing on a Gratitude Keeper card and file it in your Gratitude Keeper Kit. Do this every day for one year. Toward the end of the year, sit quietly, get comfortable, and then peel the sticker off the back of each card and carefully place each day's insight of gratitude in your Gratitude Keeper book, reading each one as you do.

Writing the daily gratitude cards identifies and hones in on that which you are grateful for. Peeling the stickers off and placing each card in your Gratitude Keeper book reinforces it and shows you that no matter what, you have 365 occurrences in your life to be grateful for, for the year on hand.

This is an exercise that makes the end of the year an even more valuable time. You'll have a Gratitude Keeper book to reflect back on for each year. Your way of viewing and living life will transform on all levels—physical, emotional, and spiritual.

First, you must to do the work, similar to your commitment to food; only this is once per day, not three or six times as having food and snacks. There's nourishment to be had on both levels—one for the physical and one for the mind and soul, which, in turn, still impact the physical.

I know that there is nothing better for men than to be happy and do good while they live...

~ King Solomon, IV- Ecclesiastes 3:12

Chapter 2
Journey with Gratitude

Giving gratitude is not a new concept, idea, or approach. For years our ancestors have translated in writings and teachings the benefits and the healing values of practicing gratitude.

In the practice of expressing gratitude, one must maintain a mindset of being positive. But if we look around us, there appear to be obvious signs of our shortcomings in practicing this ancient secret. At times we become highly motivated in doing so; it's exciting for a while, and then we lose interest or simply don't allow the time to make it part of our routine. Unfortunately, we then never reach the point where we can actually start to experience the healing benefits of the journey.

The healing benefits of practicing daily gratitude are unique to the beholder. Not everyone will get this approach or believe that it is important enough to stay committed to it. In many ways, we are conditioned to recognize special holidays as a time of thanksgiving, and in between, nothing else matters. Then for others, it may be a period of recuperation of finances splurged over the holiday period.

Of course, when someone does us favors or gives us something, the natural response is to express appreciation and thanks. However, taking gratitude to a deeper level of consciousness and bringing our awareness to it in every aspect of our being and consistently practicing it daily is not an easy commitment for many.

It takes diligent work, conscious awareness, and dedication for the full benefits to be realized.

I consider the practice of gratitude a form of art; it's where life translates into colorful formations due to the fact that you are mapping throughout your highlights of gratitude and then admiring and enjoying displays of success, peace, joy, love, and more. With the art of gratitude, there are no quick fixes or shortcuts. It's truly adapting to a way of being by adjusting to a lifestyle change that engages one's consciousness and holds one accountable to a daily surrender and willingness to stay focus in every aspect of living. So, if eating is what you are doing, then just eat; focus just on those twenty or more minutes of eating, enjoy, and savor the moment. The same hold true for anything that takes your fancy. Keep the cornerstones of gratitude in your daily living, and doors will open; newly inspired connections will blossom forth.

The daily connections you make may surprise you. It may be a piece of that puzzle to unleash your dreams and hoist you to your next adventure or possibilities, thus inspiring you with hope, vision, confidence, and gratitude to assist you in staying committed to your life's journey.

Starting may not be easy for some, but once you get started, it becomes easier to maintain. At that point, you will experience significant benefits that contribute to the daily practice of gratitude. Over time this will assist tremendously in strengthening you emotionally, physically, and spiritually, thus imparting to you the inspiration you need to continue.

As part of the course of learning, we each have our encounters that either makes us strong and more resilient or cause us to feel broken and defeated. No one said it would be easy. In looking over at someone else's path, we may think that they're not having a rougher time, and so we allow our focus to shift, taking our eyes off the prize just when we're almost there. In each of our journeys we have life lessons that can either inspire, confront the ego that's in everyone, strengthen, give hope, and or maybe all of the above.

Try not to commit to the practice of comparing yourself or your situation to others; just start with where you are from your bird's-eye view, your humble steps. Age and position are not significant; the fact that you are living is.

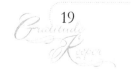

19

Guard your thoughts and keep them positive. This will signal your brain to release naturally occurring hormones needed to raise your body's cellular vibrations. In contrast, thinking negatively lowers these vibrations.

I have learned many inspiring lessons on my journey, but here I wish to share just five of those key lessons with you.

LESSON 1: DOWNWARD SPIRAL

When going through a downward spiral in life, as much as you are loved by friends and family, there's really nothing that they can do for you. Why? Because the journey is yours to experience, and so the fall must happen either to teach us a lesson, have us change the path we are on, strengthen our inner child, clip our ego, or help us to soar higher—even have us discover something amazing about ourselves or life. For me, one of those things happened. The course of my life changed. I learned how to express gratitude and wanted to share my approach with as many people as I could who would just get it.

LESSON 2: HOW ARE YOU?

When people asked me, "How are you?" I realized something interesting. When I answered that question truthfully with any answer other than, "Fine. How are you?" the majority of the people didn't care, and many found a distraction to block listening. As a result, I learned to share only as necessary and to always remember that not everything was about me.

Now when I'm asked, "How are you?" I try to share at least one aspect of life that I am grateful for, which, in essence, will lift the spirit of others so my burden or unhappiness does not necessarily become theirs. I may share how beautiful the day is, the brightness of the moon the night before, or how amazing the stars are at night; the strikingly beautiful colors of fall; or maybe how magnificent the snowfall has been. There are so many things to tap into, and based on each of our experiences, our conversation will vary.

LESSON 3: CONTROL

We each have that control to change our situations to a better outcome. With that said, I realized I could control the bad feelings inside me and instead think on good things. We have control to make our lives the best they can be. We have the control to make changes that allow the positives in us to outshine. We are the controller of our dreams.

LESSON 4: ALWAYS A LESSON

When a situation arises that we believe is not favorable to our circumstance, we become agitated, fearful, disappointed, and doubtful of life. At that moment, it's difficult to step back, take an objective view, and examine how that situation has led to other things. It may be the introduction of a particular person or persons in your life, or some other decision that was made, as a result of being able to see things, from a different perspective, after some time has passed. As unfortunate as the original situation may have been, that situation may have challenged you to become better or change your path.

The bigger picture never seems to be in full view until circumstance and time pivot us there. I compare this to flying above in an airplane looking down through the window. The view from above definitely changes perspective on life and reinforces the fact that there is still a greater force in our lives. Therefore, within each day we are blessed with, we play our part well with conviction and confidence by doing all that we can. The rest is divinely orchestrated.

As bad as things may seem, there is always a lesson to learn and strength to be garnered and embraced. In every life lesson there is still light and hope if we just adjust our view—in some cases just a tad. So live for today, but be prepared when tomorrow comes—ready with a pen in hand, because there's always a new page to write.

I'm not here just for material gains, or for myself, but to be of service in ways that uplift humanity and embrace higher levels of life frequency. When we come to realize that we are energy beings in physical bodies, it should change the way we view life. It should change our relationships with each other and also the way we choose to communicate.

At this level there are no prejudices, no color, and no power struggles. Here the human connection is real. From the sky above to the earth below and all around, the energy of light, love, and purity synchronizes with our energy and feeds and sustains it.

These life lessons that I learned offered me the impetus and inspiration to design Gratitude Keeper. Gratitude Keeper is a magnificently arranged approach geared to help one reflect on the happenings in life where gratitude is not often recognized and expressed. It's a participation tool that serves as a reminder and offers affirmations and encouragements on how to be grateful.

It encourages the spirit of being grateful daily for just one thing that you might otherwise take for granted or not ascribe gratitude to—like the pleasure in a cup of coffee, a child's laughter, a spouse's supportive touch, a smile from a stranger, a bird at the feeder, or an outing with a friend. There is just so much. When you look for things to be grateful for, I guarantee you'll find them. Moreover, they will accumulate on your countenance, and you'll find your own happiness.

Strength does not come from winning. Your struggles develop your strengths. When you go through hardships and decide not to surrender, that is strength.

—Arnold Schwarzenegger

Chapter 3
My First Awakening

As a natural practitioner, I have studied the art of finding the right medicine to address particular symptoms and concerns presented to me by a client and with significant success.

One of few types of medicine I would prescribe was homeopathy. Homeopathy is recognized as the second largest system of medicine and is used in countries worldwide. It has also been stated to have been the medicine of choice for the British royal family for almost a century.

As a result, I have been regularly consulted by clients suffering from multiple health challenges who needed my assistance to get past their emotional blockages. I'm honored that I have been able to assist each one, either through direct treatment or by referring them to another practitioner.

I've been privileged to meet people from diverse backgrounds, and I've listened to their stories of despair, disappointments, depression, and anxiety. I eagerly wanted to understand more of their influences and experiences that created their paths and then to discover ways in which to assist their healing and impart a positive impact in their lives.

So, I embarked on a soul-searching journey to closely examine my true purpose. During this journey, I was troubled by some very tough challenges and questions. I later discovered I could relate to a few of those familiar tendencies associated with similar health challenges my clients had presented in the past.

I decided in an instant that there were lifestyle changes I needed to address—changes to impart better awareness, enlightenment, and strength to maneuver my life in a different pathway. Then the unexpected happened …

For me, it happened like this:

My husband and I settled into a beautiful beach home he had renovated for our comfort. The view was spectacular. The water served as the backdrop for the entire house. I miss those breathtaking sunrises. They served as an amazing beginning to my day and an incredible reminder that we are of an intelligent design—a higher power—and we are definitely here for a purpose greater than self.

For the years we lived there, I cannot call to mind two sunrises ever being the same. I recollect whispering to myself repeatedly, "How magnificently creative and colorful our Maker is." There were so many memorable days of enjoying the view and the serenity of the water. Then inside the house we felt the warmth of the fireplace and shared delightful food with friends and family on special occasions.

I recall vividly splendiferous sunny-day walks on the beach, savoring the fresh air and feeling the rhythmic churning of the sand about my feet as I walked and picked up rocks. I would then use these rocks to accent my art adventures on canvas. Each walk was such a delightful experience that effervescently awakened all my senses and transformed my sense of being.

One particular summer it was as though the cards of life had been shuffled vigorously and then a strong wind moved in and displaced them all, but not in my favor. Then simultaneously, our once-successful business crumbled, my eldest son, Sirsean, was seriously injured in a car accident, and I lost a sister and two best friends to cancer.

The financial commitments that were needed to support these unexpected events sent my husband and me into a financial spiral. It was a horrible space to be in at that time of my life. Mere words could not express the energy of instability and fear that dominated.

I couldn't find "that" safe place in which I could turn to for help; there was no one I spoke with who made me feel that they were listening. I went on to develop a very comforting relationship with food and thereby indulged in self-pity and gloom; tears came quickly. Every door we knocked on for help directed us deeper into a financial nightmare with high interest rates and extremely high closing costs.

I found myself at a point where the mortgage payments could not be met, and everything dwindled away in a flash. Just when you're not expecting it, the rug gets pulled from underneath you. Then what? With my son in intensive care still fighting for his life, this truly brought me to a very humbling and vulnerable point.

Then I asked myself the question: What lesson can I possibly learn from this horrible circumstance? Time shifted slowly, and my breathing became shallow. I was aware that I wasn't breathing properly, but somehow that was not what was important at the time. We waited anxiously but patiently in anticipation of the news regarding the severity of his injuries. Then incredible news came in—just what we wanted to hear: "His spine is clear of any injury." Wow! How powerful and such an incredible blessing. "He will recover completely, but due to the head injuries, he will endure some challenges that he will overcome with time."

After being in the ICU on a breathing machine, his slow recovery was a miracle. I was grateful for the small successes in his improvement. My husband and I, along with Sirsean's brother and sister, took turns assisting with his care, which was 24/7. We stayed by his side for a few months. I could now breathe a big sigh of relief, and joy filled my heart once more when it was fully realized that he was going to recover completely.

A few months passed, and I was still struggling with that financial downward spiral. The lawyers who handled my son's case gave us the bad news that there was no compensation for what we had spent toward his care. This was because the driver of the car in which he was a passenger had insurance but not a valid driver's license. *This is not good*, I thought. *But most importantly I'm grateful he's alive!*

Gratitude
Keeper

The financial challenges became unbearable, and the light at the end of the tunnel people talk about just seemed completely out of sight. The predicament I was in started to unravel swiftly out of control, and I felt helpless. I hated moving; I hate packing boxes, uprooting, and putting it all back together again.

I imagined that we would have continued to enjoy the peaceful view and the amazing ambiance of the water. But no, there was definitely another plan—one I had yet to become acquainted with. The mortgage payments could not be met, and the mortgagers' need their money or the home. The morning the sheriff came to lock the doors, locking us out of the lovely home we had purchased, renovated, and enjoyed for a few years, was devastating.

It was unbelievable, disappointing, and hard to take in; we were downsized from 3,800 square feet to a car. I can only smile now when I reflect back, thinking how unpredictable life is and how hilarious it was to be in such a position. Funny, I laughed, thinking to myself that there should be insurance policy for a position such as this.

Sometimes things happen in a flash, and you ask yourself a question or two. Is this for real? Is this happening to me? Or you may even ask, why now?

When it all happened, it took about a week before I could really feel the intensity and emotional crush of it and realize the impact on a whole. Of course, at that point I could only see the negative angle and all the shame and blame. Pride superseded in terms of me showing any vulnerability. I was defiant in maintaining a happy and cheerful disposition, which made the muscles of my face and neck ache like crazy. As a result, smiling became a painful ordeal for me. With my knowledge, education, and experiences, I felt like I was reduced to the size of a pea— inadequate, lost, unaccomplished—and I felt like I had failed, failed myself and my family.

Soon thereafter when someone asked me how I was, I would respond fumingly, showing shadows of hopelessness, fear, and disappointment, not consciously aware of the impact of my responses. Seemingly self-centered qualities came darting through.

All that one may seek at such a point is either physical comfort, understanding, a loving embrace, direction, or sometimes just a listening ear. Of course, in many cases, as was true in my case, all of the above mentioned would have sufficed.

Instead, I often received a: "Hi, Maxine. How are you?"

I'd respond: "Fantastic! Thanks … Yourself?"

Only to hear back: "Great."

I didn't want that superficial touch and get away fast before anything else is said. Does that ring a bell?

Have we given ourselves quality time for conversations? Do we even care? Are we asking just to be courteous, or has it become a habit of speech? Maybe it's our preconditioning? Whichever one it is, we are still the controllers of our speech and action. It should mean something significant to us.

After experiencing several traumatic life challenges, this was the breaking point for me. I realized right there that I still had much learning, emotional strengthening, and discoveries on the way. However, the one key thing I learned in that dreary part of my life was gratitude. Despite my son's injuries and losing our home, yes, I learned Gratitude! Gratitude! Gratitude!

Those harsh realities brought me to a daunting halt and helped in my awareness to raise the frequency of my consciousness, thereby improving my state of being.

I found myself reflecting back on the clients I had attended to in the earlier years of my practice—the ones who had intimate, familiar, everyday experiences of anxiety and depression. It gave me a chance to look at the paths that had led them to the edge and then to explore ways of first helping myself and subsequently others from succumbing to the negative elements of their lives.

Each life experience is an opportunity; it is our perception that steers it.

I observed that there are people who spend their whole lives facing conflicts and challenges of all kinds, and those become their focus. They don't only savor the good stuff. In fact, many don't even recognize the good, even when it's right there for them to see and hold, so the ugly ends up outshining the good, possibly leading to anxiety, depression, negativity, or unpleasant circumstances that create life-changing dents in both personality and character.

The art of living involves the art of learning intertwined with the art of experience. The revelations from our experiences, whether physical, emotional, or spiritual, afford us the strength to carry on and the empowerment to share.

We each represent a magnificent piece of life's giant puzzle. No matter how we rally against each other, we are connected, and each one is definitely here for a purpose. If each one rises to share, build together, and impart hope, love, respect, and gratitude, how incredible life would be. Just imagine.

Within these five key lessons I learned, I realized them to be the prelude to almost everyone's story …

Lesson 1: A downward spiral
Lesson 2: How are you?
Lesson 3: Control
Lesson 4: Always a lesson to learn
Lesson 5: I'm not just here for myself

And more …

And within the corners of our minds, the private thoughts of doubt and fear linger and disrupt the energy from flowing freely, leaving us stuck on the strong tendencies toward thinking negative, leaving us resigned to the fact that it's human nature and, therefore, expected.

Many may find it enjoyable listening to gossip of any kind, craving excitement for news, whether it's talking favorably or hearing news about someone else. It's always about it happening to someone else. As long as it occurs at a distance to us, it seeds that false sense of security.

Our natural tendency is to express joy, sadness, or even pain in hearing it.

At some point thereafter, we either take it to bed with us, exchange it around the dinner table with friends or family, or mingle it in with our quiet time. It would be great just to say that it's too violent to watch or that we don't wish to hear anything negative. Regardless, there's that curiosity that piques our interest and needs to be satiated. Sometimes we just can't help ourselves; our curiosity must be satisfied. Well now that we have allowed that form of energy into our minds through the channels of our eyes and hearing, now what? How do we switch it off or release it and not allow it to seep into our reality? Then the lingering question becomes, how do I let go of what no longer serves? Or it evolves into a revolving battle in the mind between the thoughts, "Can I let go?" and "Maybe I don't want to let go."

Have we carried the emotional baggage for so long that the detriments of it become a part of who we are in that we're not sure how to recognize it for what it is or the damage that it makes to our state of being? How do I pinpoint what it is? In my experience and observation, I believe that letting go of what no longer serves us comes down to the first thing that rides the mind every time you stop to reflect. Clearly, if it's not about the art of loving or being positive and productive about life, then it's absolutely for the let-it-go category!

The next question you may ask is: How do I let go without harm to me, whether emotional, spiritual, or physical, and without harm to my loved ones? This is a significant question.

It's easy for me to say let it go, but is it really that simple? We have to first simplify things, and it starts in the mind.

The mind is our strong controller, and we need to give it the instructions to let it go. You may have convinced yourself for so long that it's safe to hold on to it and that letting it go creates a void. Thus, letting go also involves giving yourself permission—permission to let go, permission to enjoy life, and permission to awaken all your senses to the realities of this here and now.

Now that you have given yourself permission, get comfortable and take three full, deep belly breaths through your nose. Hold each one to the count of five, or as comfortable for you as possible, and then release through your mouth.

Try to make the conscious effort to focus on the rhythm of your breathing. Pay specific attention to those three full breaths before returning to your normal breathing pattern.

Now repeat the following:

>	My mind is healthy. My body is healthy.

>	Every organ in my body is healthy.

>	Every artery, vein, and capillary in my body, is completely free of blockages, free of debris, and free of plaque. My circulation is perfect.

>	All 206 bones in my body are healthy, normal, and strong.

Every cell in my body has all the nutrients and electrical charge needed to keep me healthy and perfectly balanced.

Mentally, emotionally, physically and spiritual. I am Prosperous, I am Victorious, I am Physically and Spiritually protected. I am fearless.

I now let divine love be made alive in me.

I'm beautiful inside and out, and I am spiritually very, very powerful.

I now give myself permission to forgive and release all that no longer serves me.

Thoughts of what you need to let go may flow rampantly in and out of your mind. Don't fight it. Pay close attention, and release each one as it appears. It will come again. Don't avoid it. Instead, look at it again and again and then release it. For as many times that it appears, do these exercises over and over again, and slowly, the situation will start to lose its significance and its impact on you. It's important that each time those unwanted images flow into your mind that you also take a full, deep breath with it and release with exhaling through your mouth.

Think about how grateful you are that you have the ability to be in control of your mind and your breath. You are the controller of your thoughts, and no one has the key but you.

The secret of health for both mind and body is not to mourn for the past, worry about the future, or anticipate troubles, but to live in the present moment wisely and earnestly.

~ Buddha

Now as you repeat this phrase, you may find those images and thoughts drifting in and out of your mind. Be assured that letting go gets easier with each practice. If you continue to practice this as part of your daily routine, you should begin to notice a good difference in your life and in the way you feel.

If after a while of practicing this, you still find that you are holding on to the negativity and unforgiveness, then ask yourself these questions: How is holding on to this now serving me? Is it affecting my health? Is it affecting who I believe I am? Does it affect how I react to those around me?

If the answer to these questions is yes and you are sincerely willing to let go, then you may wish to consider whether professional guidance is an option for you. This may be the missing link to assist you on this journey, and if so, it's okay.

I recalled within my first year of opening my practice that I treated a number of clients. One in particular had experienced a very difficult time emotionally, and he asked that I help him through it. It's ironic that when I asked him if he could tell me one thing that made him feel grateful, his response was, "Nothing is going well for me, and all is a shamble."

Fast-forward … Here I am now writing about gratitude.

Reflecting back, I pointed out to this client that he was sitting in front of me fully breathing and looking at me. He was hearing the questions I was asking and speaking to me. His heart was beating without his control or input. Before that, he walked in through the doors to my office.

In response, he leaned back in his chair, laughed, shrugged his shoulders, and said, "Wow! I never thought of these things. Perspective, I guess."

Of course, this will not be everyone's story. We are all uniquely different even though our created design remains the same. The human qualities and frailties that this patient got to realize were these: He could hear, see, walk, and speak with reciprocal value to any conversation, while there are many people knowingly who are not able to enjoy those blessings. Once his perspective shifted, the experience led him to recognize the important life value of being grateful. He left in a better position to apply this throughout his life on a more conscious level.

Life's journey is spiritual awareness and the peaceful feeling of oneness with the Divine.

~ Sylvia Macaulay

Gratitude Keeper

Chapter 4
The Art of Breathing

Proper breathing is a great harmonizer to the body, and it allows the lymphatic system to work efficiently in cleansing our bodies of toxins. It calms our nerves, relaxes our muscles, creates an atmosphere of peace, nourishes our hearts, rejuvenates our spirits, and is the first sign of life.

Without breath, there is no life. Yet, it requires nothing of us. It naturally gives.

Sometimes our state of affairs puts us on a treadmill course, and there is absolutely nothing we can do but breathe—just breathe.

Allow those few moments and let breathing be the focus—that gentle intake and outflow of breath. No, it doesn't make the problem go away. However, it assists in releasing some of those naturally occurring feel-good chemicals that the brain produces known as serotonin, endorphins, and oxytocin. These are happy, feel-good, and pain-reducing chemicals that we are naturally blessed with; this will change our attitudes.

Once our attitudes have changed, this engages perspective. With this enlightened perspective, our views on any situation become entirely different, and the walls of fear, unforgiveness, anger, and whatever else we wish to throw in come down or melt away. Communicating then becomes easier and how to handle our situations becomes clearer.

Consequently, no matter where we are from, who we are, or how powerful we are financially or otherwise, we cannot exist without the power of breath. Understanding the power of breath is profound—even more so when we take our awareness to it and consciously express gratitude for it. It's nothing but powerful.

Meditation

This awakening led me to explore the art of meditation, which is practiced by many people worldwide and has been scientifically proven to improve the gray matter of the brain. This part of the brain is active in muscle control and sensory perception, such as hearing, seeing, memory, emotions, speech, decision-making, and self-control.

I believe that meditation is about developing a conscious awareness regarding one's self and environment through accentuating proper breathing techniques. It's spending time daily to connect with the inner realms of your body and then giving gratitude organ by organ. Any religious discipline should not be a factor. The power of breath sustains who we are. Therefore, the aim here is to heighten and attune our bodies' cellular vibrations through the power of breath.

This conscious awakening flows nicely into the practice of writing a daily gratitude card—a simple act that will assist in the elevation of the body's cellular vibrations and life frequency, as well as transform the power of our mind and our health. As our awareness expands, we recognize that we cannot always hold gratitude in our thoughts, and we shouldn't. It must be released to flow out like ripples on the water.

Inhale Deeply Through Your Nose.
Hold, count- 1, 2, 3- then slowly
release through your mouth.....
Release... GIVE Gratitude

Gratitude
Keeper

Chapter 5
The Power of Gratitude

Imagine the tremendous works happening within our bodies on our behalf for our highest good. It's mind-blowing and incredible.

"I praise you because I am fearfully and wonderfully made." (Psalms 139:14; NIV)

There are trillions of cells in every organ of our bodies that are highly structured and vibrantly communicating with each other 24/7 to keep our organs functioning optimally. They work from an intelligent design to sustain our breath, keep our hearts ticking, and maintain us in a conscious, functioning state each day.

According to findings translated through the ages, our thoughts invoke neuropeptides in the brain that travel to every part of the body, influencing it on a physical level. This also holds true on the emotional level. Our negative thoughts impart negative messages that disrupt our cell-to-cell communication process, creating blockages that will at some point impact our well-being, both physical and emotional. Over a period of time, as this cell-to-cell communication process remains interrupted, an unhealthy cycle ensues, contributing inertly to the deterioration of our health.

Gratitude Keeper is designed to help break through many of these blockages. Daily practice of gratitude transforms negative thoughts into a flow of positive vibrations. These vibrations will raise our consciousness, elevate the frequency of the life force, and assist in keeping us on track. Being grateful is similar to eating properly to stay nourished or diligently working out to keep fit.

This daily practice of Gratitude Keeper is an incredible tool and important to practice no matter how positive we think we are already. It's valuable to help our minds stay on a positively active track. When we fail to incorporate gratitude into daily life, it is just like saying, "I don't have to eat today. I'll just eat once a month or whenever I have time." While food nourishes our bodies, gratitude fortifies our minds and helps us sustain our bodies at an even higher vibration than we can imagine. Positive thinking is as vital to our well-being as healthy food.

Our thoughts create real, specific vibrations whether we are aware of them or not. Each one of us is designed with the power to activate these positive vibrations. If we are willing to do the work to maintain a healthy body, then why not do the work to strengthen and maintain a healthy mind? Gratitude thoughts benefit our minds, as well as our bodies.

When we start thinking daily thoughts of gratitude, we will begin to experience positive changes in our emotional health, physical health, and relationships with others near and far. It's valuable to remind ourselves that our feet do not control our brains; our brains control our feet. We are in full control of the steps we choose and the paths we venture on. In this, it's clear what our responsibilities are to self, family, and life.

Inhale deeply through your nose. Hold, count: 1, 2, 3. Then slowly release through your mouth. Release … Give gratitude.

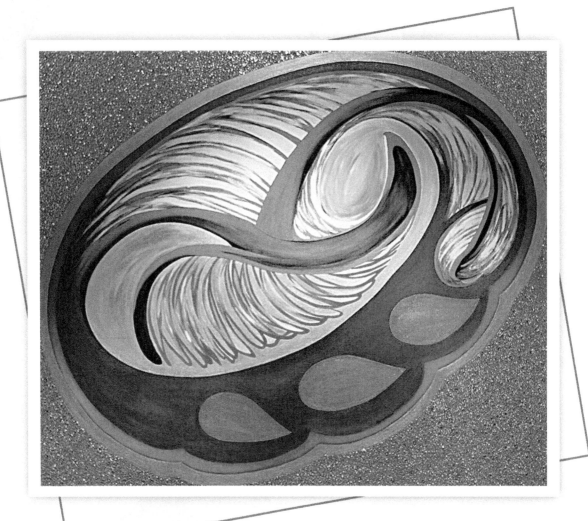

"Blessed Bond," painting by Maxine McLean

Chapter 6
Gratitude for Your Gifts

From childhood, I was raised to believe in the power of prayer. I was always encouraged by my grandmother to pray, believe, then let go. Now, I do not subscribe to any religion. However, I believe that a greater intelligence powers us, and that there is a divine plan for each of our lives. Some of us live in a way that aligns us perfectly, some struggle to find their way, and some never find that way.

The power we have in positive thinking and the power of prayer is revealed through ancient writings. Sometimes it takes going down a very tough path before we realize this power. It was granted from birth, and each of us has individual access to unlock it from within.

When we watch the work of others materialize in successes in ways we haven't for ourselves, there is no need for jealousy or envy. Each of us was given our share of gifts; we just possess different gifts with a different way of packaging, or expressing.

There is no doubt that some of us may have similar gifts. Again, it's in how we each package it. But first, your gift can only be accessed in your individual way. Remember, no one else has that access key. You can be coached, pushed, swayed, bribed—any of these and more—but if you don't turn the key, then the success of your gifts and your contribution to this life will never be realize.

Of course, it's okay to be enamored and encouraged by someone else's successes and to express gratitude and joy; however, remember that we all have the same entrance (we all started out in diapers), and we all have the same exit. It's never too late to explore your gifts; just have the desire and expressed gratitude. If you shelve your gifts and allow time to pass by, then it's your responsibility to recognize it and own it. Don't be embarrassed. It's your journey.

Allow your life challenges to bless and strengthen you.

~Maxine McLean

Chapter 7
Silent Steel

For more than a century, Hamilton, Ontario, was internationally known as Steel Town because of its strong manufacturing base of steel. This chapter is about my son (Sirsean) taking ownership of his gifts and taking it to the extreme. He decided that he would like to capture pictures of the city of Hamilton in the stillness of the night—hence, the name of this chapter "Silent Steel."

Sirsean recognized his gifts at an early age. Thus, he single-handedly and boldly schooled himself on mastering the art of photography among other related attributes. He is well respected by his peers for his amazing works of photography. He chose to do photography during the wee hours of the night between two o'clock and four o'clock in the morning. I cautioned him several times that I believed this to be unsafe; however, he insisted that he was fine and felt safe in doing so.

Well, I prayed that all evil be rebuked from him and that heavenly angels attend to him on his photography journeys. I prayed, believed, and just simply let go, and he continued to take pictures. According to him, it was amazing to capture the city at sleep on film and to feature the well-known Steel Town.

Two years after taking those pictures, he suffered severe injuries in a car accident in which he was a passenger. Fast-forward several months through his recovery; he entertained his lawyers with a selection of his pictures, at their request, of course.

I saw in those pictures images that were a strong indication that my prayers of protection for Sirsean were answered in that the angels that I requested did appear. Amazing! I couldn't sleep that night. I experienced chills throughout my body. What I saw in those pictures represented the angelic protection that I asked for and believed would occur. I believed and remained confident and positive about that outcome.

I'm grateful for the protection and grateful for the ability to listen to the silent voice of wisdom.

Follow your passion.
Stay true to your path. It
belongs to you only, Own it.
~Maxine McLean

Chapter 8
Time

Life reveals many opportunities to assist us in our journeys. There are times when life reveals things to us through different channels. Never pass on the opportunity to take it in, because that time will never happen again.

An interesting thing about time is that it never waits. It is not partial, has no prejudice, is not stereotypical, and is not a respecter of persons. I'm sure that with this statement you could also think of a few things that time is not. Time will never go backward or move in different directions. Time is precise, direct, and swift. Time will never repeat ever again. Once it's passed, that's it … Namaste … good-bye … bon voyage … shalom … zaijian … adios … aurevoir … vale … addio … adeus …

Time holds our dreams aspirations, and goals—time to be born, time to play, time to cry, time to love, time to heal, time to laugh, time to say good-bye. When time is used wisely, each day will grant new experiences and new opportunities. It's up to us to make something magnificent and memorable of time, because in each and every day another chance unfolds. The key is still ours, not for the asking but for the using.

~~~~

Now, what will I do with today? Will I give gratitude? How will I use every moment and make it memorable in the most positive, meaningful, and selfless way?

Chapter 9
Gratitude for Your Body, Mind, and Soul

Sometimes we allow our schedules to build up to a point where they become overwhelming. Your neck and shoulder muscle become tight, creating tension in your chest, and as a result, it restricts the flow of energy. You may experience shallow breathing and in many cases even hold your breath for short instances without realizing.

So now give yourself permission to journey with me. Allow a few minutes to bring your awareness to your breath. Be aware that the air you are now breathing is atmospherically balanced to keep you conscious and breathing with ease; take the time to savor it.

Mental note: Several times throughout the day we desire to eat, but our breathing happens without any input from us. So if we just take one short moment out of the day to pay attention as it circulates through our bodies and give gratitude, how amazing is that?

Focus now on the rhythm of the gentle rise and fall of your chest. Beautiful!

Now relax the muscles of your jaw, neck, and shoulders, across your chest, and extending down your arms and to your fingers. Relax the muscles of your abdomen and buttocks, extending down your thighs and feet to your toes. Relax, relax, relax. Let it go. Now be conscious of your entire body from your jaws to your toes.

Take your focus to the center of your eyebrows and journey over the crown of your head down your spine. Next, from the base of your spine, continue down to your feet, under your heels, and to the tips of your toes. Pay attention to the release of all your muscles as you journey.

Release, release, and again release.

Now listen keenly to your body. Can you hear your internal organs working away? Listen carefully. I am sure you can't, even though some people may claim that they can hear the beating of their own heart. However, each one of us lays claim to a body that is blessed with trillions of cells in every organ that are actively at work 24/7 on our behalf and for our highest good.

Do you acknowledge that? Moreover, we are not orchestrating any of it. Miraculous, isn't it?

All of that, which will benefit us, is to hold the space of gratitude during our waking hours. This kind of programing will automatically suffice through the hours that we are at sleep.

Now that I have your full attention, repeat the following in your mind or out loud, whichever is most comfortable for you …

- My brain is always in a state of receiving, processing, and sending signals to my body and releasing naturally occurring chemicals that are needed for my healing.

- My heart is contracting and taking in old blood and sending out oxygenated blood.

- My lymph system is traveling throughout my body, cleaning up dead cells and other debris and then taking them to the dumping stations, much like the city garbage truck going from street to street picking up trash and taking it to the dumping station.

- My pancreas is producing insulin to keep my blood sugar stable.

- My liver is extracting nutrients from my food and ridding my body of toxins of all kinds.

- My gall bladder aids in the digestion of my food.

- My thyroid regulates my body weight perfectly.

- My lungs allow oxygen into my body.

- My kidneys maintain my salt and water balance.

- My adrenals create different hormones that help my body maintain its balance.

- My list is long. However, what happens inside my body is the largest and most complex and complete production center known to man.

When we chose to exam and adjust our perspective, there is so much that is going well for us. For some of us, many of these functions may have malfunctioned either due to negative thinking, blockages, diseased cells, birth defects, or other things. However, in any circumstance, each case is unique, and there are still valid reasons for practicing gratitude.

These great works are being performed inside us—how magnificent! Moreover, they are specific to our bodies' needs. It's sometimes mind-boggling for us to grasp or even keep up with the magnitude of work that's being accomplished for our highest good. It's wonderful that we can be an active part of this miracle through procreation and/or lifestyle choices.

The daily practice of giving gratitude will assist in raising the vibrations of these amazing bodily functions, facilitating higher vibrations and renewed levels of health.

For you formed my inward
parts; you knitted me together
in my mother's womb. I
praise you, for I am fearfully
and wonderfully made.
Wonderful are your works;
my soul knows it very well.

~ ESV Psalm 139:13-14

I know that there is nothing better for men than to be happy and do good while they live …

~ King Solomon, IV, Ecclesiastes 3:12

Chapter 10
Cleansing Meditation

Imagine for a moment that your brain is the lighthouse of your body, and all your illumination begins here. To get started, you must be comfortable, whether lying down or sitting. When you're ready, take three full belly breaths and then follow the flow of your breath, holding each one for a count of five before slowly releasing each breath through your mouth.

Stay in the moment. Only focus on the gently rhythm of your breath as it flows in and out. At this moment, nothing else matters—just your breathing.

Now for five minutes, just remain calm in the presence of silence. Allow the muscles of your body to relax. Check again the relaxation of the muscles in your neck and relax your shoulders.

It's natural that different thoughts may begin to flow in and out of your mind, just like your breath flows in and then out of your lungs. Allow the flow, and then just like your breath, let go of those thoughts that are toxic to your well-being (release them). Relax and release them out and into the depths of the earth to be washed away into flowing water, never to return.

Bring your awareness to the inside of your head. Focus on the frontal portion of your head and turn on the lights. When you have that mental picture, take your awareness to the base of your head and turn on the lights. Ladies, to the right side of your head, just a finger breath above the ear, turn on the lights. Men, do the same but to the left side.

Now switch. Ladies, take your awareness to the left side of your head. Men, take it to the right of your head, just a finger breath above your ear, and turn on the lights. Your breathing remains gentle flowing, now expand your awareness to the very top of your head and turn the lights on.

Now that you get the vision that all your lights are on, bring your awareness to the fullness of these lights that illuminate brightly. Allow the flow of these lights to merge into one ball of brightness. Watch closely as it journeys inward, from your head and throughout your body to the tips of your toes, purging negative thoughts, negative emotions, diseased cells, and all that no longer serves you.

Now use the fullness of your imagination to sense your body. Where there is discomfort let there be comfort. Where there is weakness, let there be strength. Where there is tightness let it feel like the puff of feathers. Where there is pain visualize and allow this light to penetrate and absorb it.

Allow your imagination to follow this bright light as it passes out through the tips of your toes and continues on into the depths of the earth. Beautiful. It is done.

At this moment, give thanks to *our creator* for your presence here on Earth. How grateful you are for the positive vibrations of your brain, the electrifying energy of your breath, and the intelligence of each cell in your body.

We are shaped by our thoughts; we become what we think. When the mind is pure, joy follows like a shadow that never leaves.

~ Buddha

Visualize the formation of your brain and how magnificently wired it must be to connect with all your nuances and the frequency of each organ in your body, communicating messages to and fro with pinpoint accuracy, organization, and speed. All while only requiring from you that you maintain a diet to keep it nourished and positive thoughts to keep tuned in to a much higher frequency.

Your brain processes billions of thoughts daily. I call this the supreme processing center that operates 24/7; there is nothing like it throughout the entire universe. How amazing is it that each human being owns one—our very own communication and processing center. How spectacular is this?

Now bring your awareness to your head and take a moment to expand inward to the fullness of your brain. Get that clear image in your mind of its intricate mapping and formation. Then, when you're ready, repeat three times: My brain is healthy and magnificently wired for greatness, and I am the only one responsible for accessing its full potential.

We are each uniquely designed, even though our body parts share like features and commonalities. There are those essential characteristics that we don't share, such as our footprints, fingerprints, retina of the eye, or even the number of hairs on your head. No one will ever walk in your steps or have your experiences no matter how similar to the naked eye they might appear.

Your journey will always be unique to you. With that comes a responsibility. The question should follow: What is my purpose, here and now? Am I truly here for a reason? Now watch out! Because in the moment that you ask these heart-searching questions, things will soon begin to align in your life in favor of you and your hidden desires. Your purpose and the answers will gradually unfold as you are ready to receive and to commit. Your thoughts will become clearer, and the light to your path will unmistakably become brighter. You won't miss it.

If you already recognize that you are on your intended path, then it will only get better. However, don't think for a moment that because you are on a path that you believe is your right path that it's always going to be rosy and wonderful. Challenges will still be there in one form or another. Don't be fearful of these challenges. If you allow, these challenges will only strengthen and bless you and continue to serve as a guide and light on your life journey.

Now with grace and gratitude, bring your awareness outward and in tune with your natural rhythm of breathing.

Inhale deeply through your nose.
Hold, count: 1, 2, 3. Then slowly
release through your mouth.
Release … Give gratitude.

Chapter 11
My Second Awakening

Out from the coils of our mothers' wombs to the individuals that we've become, we've journeyed past the sperm and the egg. Have you wondered beyond and wondered if there is more to this vast universe that holds so many wonders, intrigue, and secrets? It's a mystic question that has so many variations in answers. Are you tormented with which one to place your trust in?

In spite of that, here we are on a journey that holds so many promises, adventure, dreams, possibilities, and hope. And within this vast sphere that we occupy together, we are vulnerable and fragile, yet strong. Even though we have the same entry and exit to life, our journeys remain unique and significant. Now that we have the awareness that we are who we are, we know the exit is sure. But in between there is living, planning, dreaming, exploring, and learning.

We get to learn about who we really are. Did we have a life before? Is there another reality? We are trying to understand our purpose here and now, trying to get along. Whatever the questions are, it doesn't matter. Or does it? We burden ourselves with so much, and we appear to handle everything just fine, but the one thing that we appear to struggle the greatest with is the good-bye that comes with death, or what I call a death-bye.

Many of us prepare for success, marriage, birth, and many other celebrations. But we appear to struggle when it comes to death. We struggle with letting go, and we live and enjoy life not really facing the consequential exit to this life—death. There is nothing bad about the word by itself, but just the power and energy that we ascribe to it that makes it seem lonely and gloomy. Could it be the significance that we attach to it that makes it so final and painful?

I know I have left you with many questions, but they're not for me to answer. Who am I? I'm just like you, also in search of truth love and light.

When you're a child, you're busy with play. As a teenager, it's still more fun. Early in adulthood, we are in pursuit of a career and finding ourselves and happiness. There is no time for the thought of death until it happens, and death-byes become a reality that we don't wish to have in our reality of life.

Then we come to realize that without breath, there is no life. Once there is life, death is inevitable. You're reading now, and your thoughts are running wild. Maybe you are one of those people who have anxiety or fear surrounding death. If so, let's work this through together. Stay with me here. If you're not fearful, then great! Your boldness and fearlessness will compliment and add courage.

So for the fearful, I assure you that I do understand letting go is never easy. Saying good-bye in any language always tears at the heartstring. I truly understand. In this chapter I want to share a bit of my fears and experience on death-byes.

Of course, we are all entitled to our different views and feelings, and of course, I respect them all.

I believe that while we have the gift of breath, it's an opportunity to make things right with each other and to live life to its fullest. Enjoy and celebrate the good times, and allow the bad times to teach us a lesson or two. Take some chances at making life-defining choices before it's time to say final good-byes.

As part of our life journeys, we have many relevant questions. A few journeying questions could be: What is my purpose? Why am I here? What is my gift? Then at some point in living life, the answers become clear. Your gift may simply to be the best parent possible, the best grandparent, the best brother, or the best sister.

Eventually, we will figure it out. It's simple, and the answer is always within us whether we believe this to be so or not. It's always important to know that the answer is within.

When we can assure ourselves that we have lived well and the answers to those many journey questions have been answered and met to the best of our ability, then we will have peace with letting go—peace with death-byes. Death is just a part of life that there is no escaping. So let's attune ourselves to endure and make the best of the presence of each other with gratitude and joy. So I will continue to share a bit more of my story …

Inhale deeply through your nose.
Hold, count: 1, 2, 3. Then slowly
release through your mouth.
Release … Give gratitude

I grew up in a little village by the name of Coley Mountain on the Caribbean Island of Jamaica. In this village there was no electricity and no piped water. We used torches and lanterns for our light, and we depended solely on the rain for our supply of water. Sticks, stones, and marbles were my toys, so I learned to be appreciative and creative.

I loved living on that beautiful terrain. Our home was nestled at the foothills of a mountain—shear tropical beauty. What surrounded me were chickens, goats, pigs, cows, and fruit trees of every kind.

All of this beauty didn't stop me from having fears. I was fearful of the dark and fearful of lizards, mice, roaches, and spiders—just to name a few. I also had both fear and fascination associated with death. Why? I didn't know or understand, but I was private about it. It was my private fear.

They were many instances when I heard of someone dying in the village, and I would rush to get by their side to see if there were any visible transition from life to death. What was I looking to experience? I wasn't sure. I just wanted to see if there was a change in the room—a puff of air, or mist that ascended toward heaven—but nothing happened.

I attended funerals not by choice, but because I had to go along with family. During these services, I witnessed loud outcries of grieving—people shouting and screaming, not wanting to let go. It was an incredible experience that left me fearing death even more. I knew I had to let go of the horrible fear of death, because it's inescapable. I just didn't know how.

At the age of twelve while preparing for my daily thirty-kilometer walk to school, I decided first to climb a star apple tree in order to pick star apples for my uncle. Star apples are beautifully colored, delicious fruits. They are purple on the outside, and when they're sliced open, there is a white star in the center—simply beautiful and delicious.

This climb was one that I had done many times prior, but on this particular morning, when I reached the top of the tree, I suffered a fall from approximately forty feet high onto a rock. I

recognized what had happen before I became unconscious. I remained unconscious for a few hours and didn't have any recollection of the sixty-kilometer journey to the hospital. When I awoke, I recognized that I was surely in a hospital bed with many people in white uniforms around me. They explained my injuries to me and said I would be admitted to the hospital for several months.

Being in the hospital was such an abrupt shock to me in every way. I no longer had the freedom of movement. I was feeling tremendous pain that I could not relate to or bear. Moreover, I was in a very vulnerable position—one that made me dependent on someone for everything from feeding me to bathing me in bed to using the toilet. This lasted for a brief time, and then, slowly, I could move and feed myself, although I was still somewhat physically restricted.

I fail to find the right words to describe the physical pain and the emotional adjustment of being away from family and familiar faces. The fact that I survived such a tragic fall was miraculous. It left me breathlessly feeling grateful. As time passed, I slowly adapted to my new environment.

The nurses and doctors grew to adore me, and I became their gauze-folding little girl. On days when I was feeling good, I would fold hundreds of gauzes for them to place in the autoclave for sterilization, which they later used for their wound dressings.

However, in spite of their efforts to make me happy, there were days when I felt very lonely and sad. The distance in travel and the lack of public transportation created a definite challenge for my family to visit, and so I glorified the rare occasional visits and was assured of their connection to me because they remained true and constant in their belief and faithful prayers.

The nurses and doctors became my extended family, and so I had to surrender and allow patience and prayers to guide. Prayer became my source of strength in spite of my grieving the absence of family and movement and the glory of walking and running freely among nature and its abundant blessings.

You were given this life, because you are strong enough to live it.

~ Robin Sharma

The hospital ward I was in had only adults. Death-byes were an everyday occurrence, and next to the intense pain I experienced, it was such a challenge and very draining emotionally. Fortunately for me, my grandparents taught me how to pray, and I was already acquainted with the power of prayer being a source of comfort. It kept me thinking positive and grateful that I was still in the land of the living.

One of the power-packed scriptures that they taught me was: For God had not created in you the spirit of fear, but of power, love, and a strong mind. I repeated those words in my head, which gave me the calm I needed to fall asleep at night. Still, I was anxious about all those people moaning from their pain and dying around me. There in that space I experienced laughter, hope, love, and loneliness interspersed with pain and gratitude.

Following a few very tough months in the hospital, I was discharged with still more recovery on the way. Being out felt like a new beginning—a full breath of clean, fresh air on a bright, sunny day. I was bubbling with joy to be home and be in the sunshine again, enjoying the sweet fruits of nature.

One day, as I stood in the front yard, I was startled by loud voices that echoed from people screaming in agony as they bustled down the mountain near where I stood. *What on earth was going on?* I wondered. The short answer was that a father went to his eight-year-old son's defense and was chopped in his forehead with a machete by another parent. *How horrible*, I thought.

Now a crowd of people followed this man as he walked in the unrelenting heat of the sun with blood streaming down his face. He had approximately a twenty-five-kilometer walk ahead to the nearest help, and he was determined. He walked, and the crowd followed. My eyes glance down at the bloody trail he left on the ground.

Hours later, the news came back to the village that he had collapsed dead amid the crowd. Again, I was bothered. That entire image rested in my thoughts for many weeks. I was feeling emotional

for this poor boy who had just lost his father, seemingly in a flash. This brought me back to my fear of death, and so again I asked the question: What is this thing call death that creates such excitement for some, yet makes others sad, cry, and scream in such agony?

My grandmother explained the best she could. She explained that, "Breath is a gift from God. Breath means life. Some people lose it before it's time. Some abuse its privilege, and for some it's their time to let it go once their purpose was served."

Well, I was still somewhat perplexed, but I held on to the part that stated, "Breath is a gift." That, I imagined, was her simple way to explain it so that my young mind could understand. After my grandmother died, the impact of it was very deeply emotional for me. I knew at that point my fear had to be dealt with.

Soon after her death, I began to have reoccurring dreams of her, seemingly in a different dimension but always assuring me that she was okay. Within a few short years after my grandfather died, I had another dream of my grandmother. At this point she told me she was preparing for my grandfather because he was visiting. That was unbelievable. I didn't know what to make of that, so I didn't share with anyone.

Years later, my sister had her health challenges. Then one day she asked me: "Do you think that I am going to die?"

She had me thinking, and I wasn't answering for fear of saying the wrong thing. Finally, but reluctantly, I said, "After visiting you here today, I could leave and die, either through a car accident or some other cause."

She lay there on the bed, became very quiet with a solemn look on her face, and turned her gaze to look out the patio glass door.

During that sad, relenting explanation, it suddenly dawned on me that, *Oh! It makes sense, in a corny way, of course.* I had a brief reflection of my accident years earlier, realizing that I could have ended my journey before her. I never imagined, but I was hearing myself differently (perspective, I thought), and I got an intense moment of clarity and comfort. In that moment, I thought to myself, *Am I coming to terms with death-byes? Have I overcome the fears and the remorse of it?*

Some of us may know when we're going to die, and for some of us, it's an accident. Nevertheless, it's a journey that no matter what direction in life you're from or who you are, death is no respecter of persons, and all life ventures journey to this same exit.

It's definitely a time that will always be sad no matter what the reasoning, and especially when it happens to a loved one or even to those you just hear about. That's natural. No one has an easy time with this chapter of life. No matter how we care, show that we understand, and try to console, we can never block anyone from this grieving process. It's a process that will and must be experienced for whatever reasons, whether for enlightenment or healing.

We each grieve differently. Sometimes it's out of respect, love, honor, or loss, while in other instances, it's out of fear or even guilt. It's never an easy time, and the circumstances surrounding the loss may determine the intensity to which we grieve. Even though we are aware that we are only here for a time, accepting the finality of it still doesn't make it easy to bear. The pain is real, and the loss is significant.

Thus, if we can nurture emotional and spiritual strength to help switch our perspective on death to align with our gifts, stay positive, and look around for a streaming light of gratitude, then the process of accepting and letting go will be somewhat easier. Remember that it's now part of our journey to embrace the rich legacy that was shared and express gratitude for the enlightenment to carry on before it's our time to let go. I remembered when talking to my sister that I could clearly

see the image of standing in a lineup. She was ahead of me, but I still remain in that lineup, not because of choice but because it is what it is—life.

Take heart my friend, besides eating defecating, breathing and jiving to the rhythms of our heart beat, death is every ones common pain, inescapably.

Warning: Life is fragile; handle it with care, respect, and gratitude.

~"A dedication and love to the memory of my dear sister, Constance Alegra Malden"~

*We never know when
our life journey will end;
therefore, it's important
to live life with purpose.*

~Maxine McLean

Chapter 12
Stay Present

ive life with purpose. Be with purpose, commune with purpose, drink with purpose, and talk with purpose. How many times have you locked your door, home, or car; turned off the stove; or put out the lights? Then later question yourself a million times: Did I? Or didn't I? Then you spend time retracing your actions, and in some cases, you may wonder if you're losing your mind. If this sounds familiar, then I hope you will embrace what I'm about to suggest. It's simple. Stay present. Stay in the moment. That's not easy, is it?

Despite our best intentions, the reality is that the mind can only engage one task at a time. Often we are guilty of overtasking it. We place so many things on a to-do list and then try to find answers for them all at once. There are so many different scenarios that I'm sure we can each relate to.

Here is just one common example of overtaxing the mind: While cooking dinner, you are problem-solving all the other things that need to be done. Your mind is already en route, attending to another task or present in a meeting. It left you at the stove a long time ago.

Later on, when your body and your mind catch up to each other, you ask yourself the question: Did I, or didn't I? Now begins the backtracking, and if you're really not sure, chances are you will end up rushing back to check the stove and see if it's really off.

Yes, we can be grateful that these magnificent brains of ours have rules of operation even though they were not created with a manual.

The brain requires undivided attention on any one task, and then it records without confusion. Thereby, the memory of any one act stays clearly defined. Yes, I will agree that we can accomplish a few tasks simultaneously due to the brain's ability to switch quickly from one task to the next, giving us that false sense of assurance.

If truth be told, when you try doing many things at the same time, how many times would you say you have to repeat doing any one of those tasks? Or that you forgot an important step in one? Or that you didn't have closure in another?

Staying in the moment takes effort and a daily, conscious awareness with a twist of self-control.

I can recall an experience some years ago when I had visited a client in her home, and she had just prepared something to eat. While she was eating, I thought it was an opportune time to introduce a conversation on an important matter. She turned to me staunchly and said, "No. When I eat, I just eat. We will talk after I'm finished eating."

I learned from this a valuable lesson. I was a victim of the old cliché. I thought we would kill two birds with one stone. Absolutely not. This was a humbling moment for me—another definable life lesson learned.

My perspective has since been altered for the better. I respect the time for eating as a humbling and grateful experience, you might say. The condition of our health is at the mercy of the foods we eat and how we prepare them.

I began to reflect on the whole process of preparing and eating foods. First, express the prayer of gratitude for the food, gratitude for the hands that prepared it, and gratitude to the ones who housed and sold it to those serving it on your table. Observe the colors and how beautiful they are. Stay in the moment, because eating for your health has many facets.

Acquaint yourself with the simplicity, eloquence, and rejuvenating capacity of nature, which provides the right balance of the foods needed by the cells of your body. In preparing and serving, bring to mind the rainbow of colors: red, orange, yellow, green, blue, indigo, and violet. Try to add in those colors into food preparation whenever possible. Each color and type food has an affinity for each organ in the body.

As you partake of the meal, concentrate on chewing moment by moment. Feel the texture on your tongue and gums, as well as the temperature. Is it warm? Is it cold? Is it hot? Is it spicy? Does it need more spice? Or maybe it's too salty? Or is it just right?

Enjoy the smell. Concentrate on the rhythm of swallowing—the feel of it flowing down your throat and each cell of your body moving directly for the feed of energy and nutrients.

Then sit in awe. Reflect and be ever so grateful that you are indeed an integral part of the experience of eating for a healthier lifestyle, because it happens over and over again.

Inhale Deeply Through Your Nose.
Hold, count- 1, 2, 3- then slowly
release through your mouth.....
Release... GIVE Gratitude

Chapter 13
The Pleasantries of Eating

Eating is pleasurable, no doubt. It unites old acquaintances and loved ones. It invites new acquaintances. It rejuvenates, restores, nourishes, and builds.

It's used to welcome life and to say good-bye to life. It's an important act that deserves our undivided attention.

It allows our taste buds to acquaint with the flavors and textures of different cultures. It's an act that invites in our sense of smell, sight, touch, and taste. It stimulates the release of naturally occurring chemicals from the brain, which nourish and heal.

The organs of our bodies are negotiating and setting priority on where nutrients are required. There is no confusion when in balance. Each organ plays its role well. We are wise to approach eating with gratitude.

From the earth below and the sun above, the communication is real and all for our sustenance and good health.

Food has its own cellular language that resonates with the cells of our bodies. Bitter foods have an affinity for the liver and gallbladder. Sweet food has an affinity to soothe the heart and spleen and calm the nerves. Greens have an affinity for the bones, hair, and nails.

Getting food to the table is a long chain reaction that is labor-intensive and involves the commitment of many. Their goal is getting that food to our tables to be rewarded financially. Then

our goal is to eat for our nourishment and sustenance. So to partake of food in any cuisine is a genuine delight, in that gratitude should weave and flow throughout that chain.

First, for the journey of the food to your plate; then the ability to see, smell, taste, feel, eat, and enjoy it; then to the production that happens within our bodies; and thus to the final stage of eliminating waste, incredible, simply incredible.

*No one will ever walk in
your steps, or have your
experiences; your journey will
always be unique to you.*

~Maxine McLean

Chapter 14
The Power and Simplicity of Water

It has been scientifically demonstrated that even water responds to the power of gratitude.

Water holds memory and intelligence. When exposed to words of gratitude, water showed remarkably beautiful colors in contrast to water exposed to negative thoughts, which showed horrible-looking dull images.

Water, as we all know, is a prized commodity. It's used for washing, cleaning, and cleansing our bodies of energy patterns picked up throughout our day. It is also vital for many other operations, including the function of the brain; the rejuvenation of thoughts; cellular repair; hydration of hair, eyes, and skin; the cleansing of the body; and the toning of internal organs.

Water removes waste from our bodies and transports nutrients and oxygen to our cells. Rhythms of water are recorded to enhance relaxation, the healing of the mind and spirit, and rejuvenate and promote mental calm.

Water is transparent, odorless, tasteless, and pure. It is the world's prized commodity and the primary makeup of all life, both complex and simple. Without water, life would not exist.

The energy in water is accessed to power electricity.

Our bodies are composed of more than 60 percent water. As a result of this, water should be a part of our daily intake and should be one of our priorities.

The cells of the body cleanse, travel, and multiply all for the betterment of our health. The lack of water and the influx of negative thoughts will place health at risk. Our organs will perish bit by bit in a pool of toxicity. Thus, it's important to pay attention to drinking the daily required intake of water and be conscientious that our thoughts are as positive as possible.

"Without water, there is no dignity and no escape from poverty."
—UN Secretary-General Ban Ki-moon, World Water Day 2011

Year after year and throughout the year, thousands of people from far and near travel to Niagara Falls, Ontario, Canada, to take in the beauty of watching the water flowing over the rocks.

Lakefront and beachfront properties attract a lineup of people willing to spend millions. They admire and enjoy the flow of water, which is enhanced by the relaxation and prestige that living close by offers.

When astronauts went on their space discoveries, water was their first indicator of life. In a mother's womb, there is no life without water. Plants wither and die without water.

Inhale Deeply Through Your Nose.
Hold, count- 1, 2, 3- then slowly
release through your mouth.....
Release... GIVE Gratitude

Gratitude Keeper

One evening I went driving to spend some me time while admiring the beauty nature had to offer. My thoughts were not in any one place; they were everywhere. It was surely one of those days when I tried to take on too many things at once, and it was all in my head.

However, one thing flowed into my mind with great clarity and was definitely set apart from everything else I was thinking. It set the rhythm for my entire day. Here is what my thoughts manifested: Water flows in one direction, and if we place a divider in its midst, chances are we will create a diversion of the flow. Nevertheless, this water will still flow in the same direction. You're never at some point going to see the water change direction and flow backward and then forward again. *How exquisite*, I thought.

Then I correlated the flow of water to our natural human tendency to always go back in the past and allow old hurts to become new again. When this happens, we become stagnant in one way or another: emotional, physical, or spiritual.

If we observe the flow of water and the passage of time, we can see they're both moving forward and constant, never going backward. As humans, we have adopted many lessons from nature. Could it be that there's a lesson here for us? In contrast to the flows of water, if there is stagnation in life, then it's important to work diligently to remove the cause, and thereby the obstacles. Clear away the thoughts that causing the burden and making it difficult to keep moving forward. Remove blockages—physical, emotional, and other. Release them all.

First, you have to make the decision to let go. Once that's clear, then the process of letting go begins. Keep in mind the flow of water; our lesson here is not to stay stagnant in our thoughts or situation.

If the state you are in is not offering the blessing that you were born in this life to embrace, then clearly you must let *it* go. Let *them* go. Release! Release! Release! Don't forget to cry, and if you find yourself crying, don't be ashamed and hold back the tears.

Like the motion and freeness of the river, your tears need to flow. It's an important aspect of letting go. It's one of the body's natural ways of releasing emotional toxins and giving your brain a way to release naturally occurring aids that soothe, heal, and pacify.

Practicing daily gratitude will give you an extra edge on rejuvenating your body and change your health for the better. It's a win-win.

Chapter 15
The Unseen Power

I've come to realize that prayer is a significant factor in life's journey. When we blend the power of prayer with determination, reverence, positivity, faith, and gratitude, there is no telling the miracles and personal transformation that are possible. Prayer makes us accountable to a higher power. It offers a daily feel of protection, rejuvenation, and the solaces of forgiveness, peace, and a relationship with a higher power—a higher power of which teachings we are given through ancient manuscripts.

Prayer had always been an important recharger in my life. It became the approach to my day, the closing of my day, and the continued protection while I lay vulnerably asleep. I have had many remarkable experiences with the power of prayer, and I'm sure that you may be able to write a page or two on your own experiences.

It had been my practice that as soon as I got into my car and behind the wheel, I would engage in the power of prayer and ask for guidance and protection. That's what I did on one particular morning as I set off with my daughter to visit my older son in another town. It was the middle of winter, and my daughter and I were returning from a trip to visit my son. We were traveling in the fast lane on the highway. It was very busy, and the traffic was moving swiftly.

Then … "Ouch!" I exclaimed. My car had suddenly touched on an icy patch that launched us into a whirlwind spin in the middle of the highway. We were spinning fast, and then for just a few short moments, it seemed as though everything was paused. I had the opportunity to turn to my daughter, who was in the front seat, and said, "Brace yourself, because we're going to slam into that concrete meridian. When we do, the entire front of this car is going to fold in and crush us." When I said that, there was such a powerful presence of peace and absolute fearlessness.

Within seconds of speaking, we slammed head-on into the concrete and spun back out in the middle of the highway with brute force still spinning out of control. Then the car came to an abrupt stop, facing the oncoming traffic.

It was quite an emotional and physical jolt. As we looked up to see the state we were in, to our amazement, there were no cars around us, and still no cars were coming. My thoughts to this were, *Where did all those cars disappear to?* We had just been driving in a heavy flow of cars. I turned to my daughter and said, "I guess we better get out of the way."

I had enough time to turn the car around on a very busy highway, still with no cars in sight. As soon as we were facing the right direction and had pulled off onto the soft shoulder, all the cars began coming. The flowing of traffic resumed at full force.

I again turned to my daughter and whispered, "I guess we better get out and see the damage." We stepped out of the car on the safe side to examine any damages.

After inspecting the car and realizing there was absolutely no damage, we returned to sit inside the car and could not believe what had just taken place. We were speechless, but all and all, I was left with a deep sense of peace. It was an incredible experience that I will never forget.

Reflecting on this incident, I think of the impact the car had on the concrete meridian and the fact that the highway was busy with a steady flow of traffic. I must admit that I'm limited in words to describe what that truly felt like. I was definitely in shock, but still feeling a strong sense of gratitude.

Even though it had happened to me, it all just seemed unreal and unbelievable; therefore, I didn't share it freely. The impact of it came and went, and life continued. However, when my son had his accident, faith brought me back to recognize and again employ the power of prayer and gratitude.

Years later, while I was on my way out of town, the unknown call came in from the hospital on my cell phone. "This is Dr. … from the emergency department. Is this Mrs. McLean?"

"Yes?" I answered.

"I have your son Sirsean here in critical condition. He has been in a car accident."

My heart pumped fast, my breathing was shallow, the heat began rising to my head, I felt weakness in my knees, and there was a slight blurring to my vision. "Is he going to live?" I responded.

"We are working on him. How quickly can you get to the hospital?" the doctor asked.

"I'm on my way."

Of course, the doctor tried to give me words of comfort for the journey: "Drive carefully. It will all be okay."

I arrived at the hospital to see him unconscious and on life support. Yes, of course, for just a few moments, I was fearful, but very quickly, I had to send fear for a hike and ask positivity, faith, and hope to step in. Surely enough, that was what happened.

I approached his bedside with a firm, positive energy, faithful that he was going to be okay. I whispered in his ear prayerful words of healing and gratitude, and I was fully assured that somewhere in there he was hearing me, and the cells of his body were at work by the grace of God, repairing the damages.

Months later, he had a full recovery. I'm grateful, and as much as the experience was of a difficult impact and challenge, it brought my son and me to a humbling place of gratitude. I learned for

sure that day that as humans we are ever so fragile. Life is truly unpredictable, and in a flash everything could change. Subsequently, all hopes and dreams could become a living nightmare.

There are so many situations we have no control of—whether the sun rises, the colors of the sunset or sunrise, or our waking after sleeping.

It's wise not to live life in the realm of fear, doubt, or negativity. This will surely paralyze us mentally and emotionally from achieving our life goals. For all that we have control over, keep holding on to all the possibilities of life. Never forget that we are in this life at this time because this is our place to be, and we are here for a purpose.

Recognizing that purpose is the key. Each of us must take back our power to live life fully and for the betterment of mankind in a positive and uplifting manner. Take the gift of life and hold it in your hands—dream it, see it, and now live it.

Every thought and expression of gratitude leaves an imprint on your countenance and character. Stay in the moment so you do not miss it. It will be in the eyes, the forehead, the smile, the touch of your hands, and the eloquence of your voice.

Inhale deeply through your nose.
Hold, count: 1, 2, 3. Then slowly
release through your mouth.
Release … Give gratitude.

Take a moment and expand
your awareness to your entire
body. Be conscious of your
breathing, then give Gratitude
for the power of breath.

Chapter 16
The Making of Gratitude Keeper

The moment that I thought of the material to make the boxes, there were no challenges or conflicts in my mind. It was clear that it needed to be some sort of stone that was easy to work with. Soapstone became the material of choice. I loved the idea of using soapstone for many reasons. Its name is derived from its soapy feel and talc-like softness that makes it pliable to carve, along with the following points …

1. It offers electromagnetic protection, which is useful in any environment.
2. It's a wonderful gift from Mother Earth, bearing ripples of earth's vibrations.
3. It's durable, strong, and solid; plus, it features nicely in any home décor.
4. It has healing values.
5. Soapstone's heat- and stain-resistant properties make it an ideal place to store your Gratitude Keeper cards.

As more ideas for Gratitude Keeper flooded my mind, the creative flow would often wake me up from sleep or hit me while I was driving my car, causing me to pull over on the soft shoulder and make notes.

The next step was how to package Gratitude Keeper, adding that twist of character. This led to the term "synergy of gratitude." This means that: "Gratitude is expressed full-circle."

Gratitude Keeper is divinely inspired and a journey that's worth traveling. In each box can be found the following:

- The inspired reading of a life changer—one imbued with different flares, gifts, and abilities and who was instrumental in designing pathways that allow us choices and freedom, thus making our journey attainable and purpose-driven.
- A vial of essential oil extracted from plants that have grown in indigenous soil, making the value of it potent and true to its name.
- Healing stones from nature clad in their true vibrant colors. These are adhered to the cover of the box for easy opening.

Full circle, Gratitude Keeper is unique. It's a complete package, artistically hand-painted by people in full expression of gratitude. Included is a Gratitude Keeper pen and 365 daily Gratitude Keeper cards.

The final stage was when I had to shop around the kit to gather the opinions of my peers, friends, and other people of interest. Hands down, they all loved the idea of using the soapstone and thought that the heaviness added to the value and uniqueness of the concept as a whole. To add, if anyone chose not to use it as a Gratitude Keeper, it would still be a valuable artistic accent in their home.

There you have it—Gratitude Keeper synergy of gratitude.

Day-to-day living can be tough. We face challenges and disappointments every day. Nevertheless, the best way to get through the bad stuff is to focus on the good. If your back is sore, your job is stressful, and your kids are giving you a hard time—whatever the case may be—reflect on the important lesson you learned from a difficult experience.

All you have to do is find one good thing to write down every day to experience a positive shift in your energy.

Daily use will help you to connect with the experiences of gratitude in your life. My thought is that at the end of the year if thirty or sixty things went wrong for you, or even if two hundred things went wrong, you can handle it, because with Gratitude Keeper you still have 365 things to be grateful for.

This is an important life changer, health recharger, and mind rejuvenator. Otherwise, you will become overwhelmed with the surplus of negatives, which block you from seeing or taking in those 365 positive things.

I wish you the deepest discovery of self, the honesty and strength to face it, the wisdom to change it if you need to, and the knowledge to understand when you need to seek support to embrace or release.

~Maxine McLean

A Note from the Writer

I have enjoyed the path on which Gratitude Keeper
has taken me, and I hope that I have inspired you to live life
with gratitude and to share it through writing your
Gratitude Keeper cards, creating ripples of positive
vibrations, and bringing people of all perspectives together.

The Art of **Gratitude** is adjusting
to a lifestyle change that
engages one's consciousness

~Maxine McLean

The Gratitude Keeper Journey. Welcome!

You are now on an amazing journey to develop your very own *Gratitude Keeper Book, Volume 2*. This you may choose to pass on to loved ones when completed, thereby releasing ripples of *positive* vibrations. How empowering!

1. A portion of each purchase of Gratitude Keeper will be contributed freely toward families in developing areas of the world in addition to the Clinics for Humanity, which currently serve in more than twenty-three countries. This money provides food, education, health care, clothing, and clean drinking water.

2. Endeavor to make each day a practice of gratitude. Be sure to write it on your Gratitude Keeper card.

3. The practice of daily gratitude will raise your body's cellular vibration, creating positive changes that then affect you on a physical level.

When you have completed your first year of practicing and recording in your *Gratitude Keeper Book, Volume 2*, we would like to hear your testimony. Please send in your stories to mygratitudekeeper@gmail.com. If you would like us to post your testimony, then please include written permission to do so. Only with your written permission will we post your success journey with Gratitude Keeper.

Now you can share your *Gratitude Keeper* book with loved ones, sending out ripples of *positive* vibrations, impacting generations ahead.

The Description of Gratitude Keeper

Each Gratitude Keeper is unique and beautifully hand carved out of soapstone and hand-painted as a one-of-a-kind design.

Each kit includes:

- 365 Daily Gratitude cards—a dollar-a-day gratitude, which is inexpensive in comparison to what it can do for your personal journey, your health, and your loved ones.
- Two *Gratitude Keeper* books, volumes 1 and 2
- A Gratitude Keeper pen
- The reading of a life changer
- Gift: one fifteen-milliliter pure, unadulterated essential oil; the choice of oil will vary

The dimensions of soapstone box:
Size: 25.4 centimeters square and 10 centimeters tall
Weight: approximately 6 kilograms

Our thoughts create real specific vibrations, whether we are aware of them or not...

~Maxine McLean

Reader's Guide

Discussion points for discussion groups:

If you were given the choice between money and time, what would your choice be? Why?

Every expression of gratitude records on your countenance. What does this mean to you?

Time can be used to make money. Money will finish in time. What is the importance here about time?

Money means: food, shelter, education, health care, and, to a certain extent, freedom. How can the practice of gratitude influence this in a positive way?

What are seven key things in life that you'd be wise not to take for granted?

If you knew when your last day and your last hour of breath would be, what would you do differently?

Reflecting on your past challenges, do you think the practice of gratitude may have made a difference in how you lived your life? Moving forward, can you see that it would benefit you?

How do you explain the art of active conscious living and its importance in your journey to heal and maintain good health on all levels: emotional, physical, spiritual, and mental?

What's the correlation between time and death?

Gratitude Keeper

Conclusion

It is important to understand what our gifts are and endeavor to live life similar to how we would approach going to work—knowing that we are there for a purpose and each employee has a purpose. We each strive to be the best employee and to be recognized for our gifts and contribution to that company.

We try not to have anything negative placed on our working record, and we make concessions to get along with our coworkers, because, indeed, we would like to work in a positively charged environment where we are liked, respected, and accepted.

We are so grateful for that job, because it means shelter, food, transportation, clothes, freedom, financial security, stability, and more. So we do all that we can to protect it. Then we work earnestly and faithfully even though we know that there is an end to it; still, we do everything possible so that we will be remembered when we're gone.

Life is just that way. We are all here for a purpose. Each one of us is a part of life's giant puzzle; our parts are real, and they are needed no matter how insignificant we may feel. We must endeavor to stay within the flow of life until it's our time. When that time arrives, let's be prepared to answer a few tough questions before we release our breath to its Giver.

Questions such as: Was I grateful for my breath and all my organs that labored for me 24/7? Did I claim my gifts and recognize my purpose? Did I practice gratitude, forgiveness, and love? Did I contribute to helping humanity? Was I my brother's or sister's keeper? Were my gestures and words kind, sincere, and caring to those who graced my presence?

Know that after answering these questions, we now have the blessings, assurance, and peace to rest in the release of our breath with gratitude, surrender, and love.

*Every tree knows its season, and
when it's time, they gracefully
surrender their leaves to the wind.*

Resources

Heal Thyself by Stephen Pollitt
www.sourceenergyresearch.com

The Hidden Messages in Water by Dr. Masaru Emoto

Frame Five Media
framefivemedia@gmail.com

UN Secretary-General BanKimoon's message for World Water Day 2011 (Electronic)

Images Copyright:
Vasiliy Yakobchuk, Hongqi Zhang, Tilltibet, Mark Herreid, Dan Collier, Smileus,
Daniel Jacobus Nel, Danil Chepko, Alex Antonio Luengo Ramirez, Fabio Berti,
Oleksiy, Abidal, Witold Krasowski, Amaking, Denys Kurbatov, Iakov Kalinin,
Brijith Vijayan, Tupungato, Pavel Klimenko, Antonio Guillem, Vampy1,
Valentin Valkov, Wavebreak Media Ltd, Oliver Sved © 123RF.com

Painting by Maxine McLean

With Gratitude, Love, and Warmth
Maxine McLean

Acknowledgments

Special thanks to the people of the Kambere and Tabaka villages in Kenya. This project has developed into an exceptional win-win situation. When I heard of their story, I just knew that I wanted to share in their journey to access clean water and better their livelihood. These people are creative, artistic, and eager to work, so I embraced working with them.

Special thanks to all the people in different parts of the world for accepting and bearing happily with integrity, vulnerability, and openness the tasks that life has provided and also for making your commitment in making this a win-win experience.

To individuals in developed and developing parts of the world who are suffering from health challenges, lifestyle-related illnesses, and affected by natural disaster: You are all my inspiration.

I encourage everyone possible to practice with Gratitude Keeper, and together we will raise positive vibrations that will create that ripple effect that will translate in changing lives for the better and for the wealth of mankind.

Thanks to Stephen Pollitt for his insights on water and his remarkable contribution to mankind.

Breath, Grace, and Gratitude

Observe and appreciate the splendor of silence; refrain from mental and physical chaos.
Be eloquent in speech and abstain from people that are often vociferous and
impolite, as that will pollute ones spirit and cause anguish and bitterness.

Strive always to expatiate true thoughts with clarity and tranquility.
Reverence the voice of others by sincere listening, no matter
how less capable you may believe one to be
Do not miss the joy however, that you would receive from being in harmony with precious souls.
Good people are in good numbers identify and be associated with them.

You are one of a kind; uniquely designed … Refrain from comparing yourself with others
for this will only cause anguish, as there will always be
higher and lower profiles in your life journey.
Do not become an emotional miser
Remember to breathhhhh … deep and full then release with the thought that you have just
released the negative emotions, the mental pollutants and all that no longer serves you.
Vivify yourself spiritually this will help you to remain stable in times where ill fate dominate life.
Foster genuine regard for self and other forms of life

Find pleasure in the plans you make
Connect with joy and gratitude in all your achievements …

However small they may be, endeavor to Love your career … that
is your true asset in the world of waiving fortunes.
Be on the alert to identify traps and crooks in the world of
business and handle them with out-most caution.

Be your natural self, not pretentious or slow to affection but also take care not to have adverse ideas on love, love is like the rose with thorns, prevalent in all stages of life and the world. Endeavor to create a legacy built on dedication, honor, integrity, love and gratitude.

Imbibe the wisdom earned through experience and happily let go the mediocrity of young age. Do not conjure fearful thoughts in your mind, this only leads to distress and anxiety. Ensue self-discipline, practice gratitude and stay focus on your goals.

The universe is evolving swiftly; however, be assured, that like the trees and the stars you have all the rights to live this life in abundance.

Time holds all dreams, aspirations and goals; so be open minded to discern, embrace and live.

Unearth Divine Wisdom and embrace truth and light; even though your daily chores may be amidst acoustic chaos, do not stray away from the inner solace of the "Soul"

The world may have blemishes of treachery and one's achievements may appear slim, or dreams never realized, take courage, it's a magnificent world and if you manage it with care, practice gratitude, spiritual respect and love, it's limitless what can be achieved. Every tree knows its season and when its time they gracefully surrender their leaves to the wind.

~ Adaptation by Maxine McLean

The above poem is inspired by "Desiderata" by Max Ehrmann.

Namaste, my friend …

Lightning Source UK Ltd.
Milton Keynes UK
UKOW07f2356071217
314058UK00005B/22/P